# Nature and me

Sumaiyya Patel

BookLeaf Publishing

India | USA | UK

Presentation by *BookLeaf Publishing*

Web: www.bookleafpub.com

E-mail: info@bookleafpub.com

ISBN: 9789358319750

First edition 2023

# ACKNOWLEDGEMENT

Acknowledgement to my English Teacher Mrs Rodriguez, who encouraged me to continue in my writing and learning journey, as she saw potential in me.

# Walker

The wind is blowing
My feet gently swaying too
I'm a wind walker

# Words

Words oh words
They have the power to heal
With harsh tones
They have the power to steal

They can steal joy
They can allow a ploy

Words oh Words
They have the power to heal

They can cause happiness
And bring out Sadness

They can give solace
And allow you to promise
They can make history
And set aside misery

Words oh Words
They have the power to heal

They have the power to ignite
A fire from within

They have the ability ,
to give comfort
Through words, our strength and agility,
 we can assert

Words oh words
They have the power to heal

# Grounding meditation

Breath
Thought
Posture
Comfort
Dis-comfort
Acceptance
Noticing
Changing
Acknowledging
Ground-breaking
Ordinary
Focus
Re-focus
Just being

# Grounding (acrostic)

Grounding yourself with gravity
Resting in one motion
Omitting negative thoughts
Under minimum influence
Noticing your thoughts and feelings
Do not disturb
Ignite something from within
Noting any changes or feeling
Grounding yourself with gravity

# Hope

Happiness is fleeting
Overcome your obstacles
Praying for better, with
Everlasting faith

# Hope 2

Happiness
Orange and Yellow canvases
Pretty petals
Enriching my life

# Admiration

Why would we admire something
Is it because it's shiny
Or cool
Or loveable
Or is it because it benefits us
Why would we admire something?

Is it beacause it's something we don't have
Or is it because we like this thing

What's actually more worthy of admiring
Is the true beauty within
The resilience we have in hard times
And the strength we have within
What's also worthy of admiring
Is the gruelling hours someone puts in
And also the natural talents a person is born with

What's worthy of admiring
Is the beauty of this world
And the creator of all this.

# The Voyage

Mountain tops
Peaks so high
Earth bellow
Like a pillow

Wind blowing agust
My hair doing the most
Wind in my face
I tie my shoelace

I walk to the station
In one motion

People walk and scurry
I wonder if they're in a hurry

Trains come and go
Platforms and rows

Now we're back to the mountains
In my mind
So tall and majestic
Not a care in the world at all

# Fear

Fascinating
Endangering
Analysing
Rare

# Shells

Shining sea shells
Lying on the cold dark beach
Who knows their story?

# Change

Change is inevitable
Change is necessary
Change isn't always pleasant
Change isn't very ordinary
Change can be exciting
Change is what I need

# Blackpool

Bright lights
Long pathways
Angelic views
Cars and coaches
Kids and family
People everywhere
Overlooking shores
Over the top costumes
Loud and crowded hustle and bustle

# Rain (Haiku)

Rain falls lightly
Tip tap on the surfaces
My heart attunes

# Life

Life just is
Inevitable for us to be living
Filling up the void with anything
Engrossed in matters that may or may not help.

# Fear and Hope mashup

F-fearing failing but
H-honesty is the best policy
E-everything can go wrong but
O-opening offers are here
A-anxiety about what will happen
/anxiety around doing a task
P-perfection is not necessary
R-rail in your fear
E-everything will work out

# Fear

Fear is feeling timid
Earning the doubt of others
Anxiety around doing a task
Running rampage in my mind

# Nature in the park

Pretty petals fall on the ground
Leafs rustle and crunch beneath my feet
The wind blows ever so softly
The trees sway side to side
All of nature in perfect harmony

Squirrels rush around
Nowhere to go, fearful of people
Scurrying between branches and tall trees
I lose myself amongst the trees
All of nature in perfect harmony

I see, long and short pathways
Leading me to different destinations
Some paths merge into one
The park is like a map,
Leaving trails to be followed
All of nature in perfect harmony

# My Niece

Small feet but big boots to fill
You never fail to uplift us when we feel down
You turn our frown, upside down
You ask questions with curiosity
You are inquistive about many things
You always lift my heart and make it feel like a
butterfly
With your innocence, you allow growth
You allow goodness and you bring out the best
in me
Your demands can be many
But I have to shun them with wisdom
You are only small
But you hold a big part in my heart